LOVE POEMS

Love is the poetry that life writes in our hearts

Written by Creag McMillan
Illustrated by Heidi Sturgess

LOVE LIST

2	Never A Mistake
3	Half of My Heart
5	Love's Maths
9	Rose
11	Morning light
15	Whispered Moments
17	Where Time Stands Still
21	Between Breaths
23	Roses Speak
27	Tu es ma Belle
29	Your Charismatic Light
33	Her Birthday
35	Let It Go
39	Passion's Embrace
41	Her Rhythmic Soul
45	Dancing Through Difference
47	Days Upon Days
51	Unrequited
53	Not Sorry For Love
57	Continental Drift
61	Dreams Beneath Northern Skies
65	The Perfect Mistake
69	Secret Yawning
73	You Pause Me
77	The English Exit
78	The French Exit
81	The Light You Bring
83	To My Poem for You
85	The Recycling Crisis
87	This Tale Will Never Get Paroled
89	Time's Sacred Scroll
91	A Song of Times Past and Present
95	Left And Right
96	The Match
97	The Local Dilemma
98	Double Doors, Double Lives
99	The Gentleman's Guide
100	The Meet
101	Tuscan Sunflower
103	You Are Missing From Me

Love, as the Beatles said, is all you need. And they were right.

Never A Mistake

It's never a mistake to speak the heart,
To let words fall like autumn leaves—
Honest, vulnerable, true.

For even in the trembling moment
Before response, you've honoured
What lives within you.

Regret lingers longer than rejection;
Silence weighs heavier than any answer.
The words not spoken haunt us most.

So let your truth take flight—
A bird released from careful hands,
Free to soar or return.

For in love's economy,
Courage counts more than outcome,
And honesty outweighs perfection.

Half of My Heart

Half of my heart now lives in your smile,
Each moment pulling me further away
From everything I knew, mile by mile.
Time pauses, then flows with a gentle style,

As feelings deepen, like the dusk of day—
Half of my heart now lives in your smile.
Thoughts swirl in circles, file by file,
Unwritten stories have their say,
From everything I knew, mile by mile.

Each glance exchanged becomes a trial,
Testing the calm I try to delay—
Half of my heart now lives in your smile.
Emotions pile up, turning fragile,
While old certainties begin to fray,

From everything I knew, mile by mile.
Perhaps it's best to reconcile
That hearts will always find their way—
Half of my heart now lives in your smile,
From everything I knew, mile by mile.

Love's Maths

I calculate the angles of your smile,
Compute the gravity that pulls me near,
Plot the careful graphs of minutes we share,
And measure out our moments, mile by mile.

Each laugh's trajectory I analyse,
Each glance's vector pointing straight to heart—
These calculations, growing more like art,
As numbers dance before my wondering eyes.

What formula could map this strange delight?
What theorem proves why my pulse quickens so?
These questions multiply the more I know.

Till all equations blur in evening light—
For love's mathematics, I've come to see,
Adds up to more than one plus one makes three.

Love wants to hold someone's hand
— and never let go.

First Light

That moment when ordinary light
suddenly becomes extraordinary—
the world seen through new eyes.

Rose

Rose, love's glow in gardens bright,
Soft velvet dress kissed by the dawn.
Passion's symbol, pure delight,
Hearts adore your beauty, drawn.

Silken petals whisper strength,
Fragrant secrets fill the air.
In every bloom, you stretch your length,
Soothe the soul with tender care.

Breezes kiss your blushing face,
Petals dance and sway with grace.
Eternal in your vibrant might,
Blooming beauty, a pure delight.

In twilight's hush, your scent remains,
A whispered promise, a heart's refrain.
Yet shadows play as petals fall,
Love's bittersweet echo calls.

Morning light

Dawn filters
  through half-drawn blinds
    finding you
      in gentle stages

each ray
  discovers
    something new
      I hadn't seen before

the way light
  catches
    in your movements
      as you read
        lost in thought

morning
  unfolds
    quietly
      between us
        in soft
          revelations

your presence
  grows
    clearer
      with each
        passing
          moment

like sunlight
  spreading
    across water
      creating
        patterns
          I want to

remember

Love can make strong men weak,
And weak men weaker.

Recognition

Before words,
two souls nodding
in silent acknowledgment.

Whispered Moments

soft words
　drift between us
　　like autumn leaves
　　　Settling

in the quiet
　of afternoon light
　　I watch you
　　　lost in a book

your fingers
　trace lines
　　of poetry
　　　as if they
　　　　touched
　　　　　whispered
　　　　　　secrets

and I collect
　these moments
　　like precious
　　　stones
　　　　slipping
　　　　　into
　　　　　　my
　　　　　　　pocket

the way you
　pause
　　between pages
　　　lost in thought
　　　　finding yourself
　　　　　in words

while time
　breathes
　　around us
　　　in whispers
　　　　we've learned
　　　　　To understand

Where Time Stands Still

The way you lifted up that cup to drink—
A simple act, yet somehow time grew still.
Your fingers curved with grace I can't instill
In words, though through my thoughts they weave and link.

I hadn't meant to notice, hadn't planned
To catch that half-smile playing at your lips,
Or how the morning light so gently slips
Across your face, a moment, soft and grand.

Why should such quiet gestures hold such weight?
What makes these simple movements catch my eye?
These questions echo as the day drifts by,
While in my mind, these moments recreate
Themselves in endless loops of wondering how
Such ordinary time grows precious now.

Love makes fools of us all.
And thank goodness for that.

Surrender

The strange relief of finally letting go
of who you thought you were.

Between Breaths

In the space
  Between heartbeats
   I find
    moments of you

suspended
  like motes
   in morning light
    in morning light
     Dancing

between each breath
  time stretches —
   elastic
    infinite
     yet intimate

the way silence
  holds music
   in its palm
    before notes
     begin

I've learned
  to live
   in these spaces
    where seconds
     pause
      and wait

while the world
  around us
   continues
    unaware
     of how time
      bends

Roses Speak

The garden stirs in whispers as the morning wakes,
Each rose a secret promise that the daylight makes.
Their petals catch the sunlight like a soft caress,
As time between each heartbeat slows, in quietness.

Such beauty asks no questions, yet answers fill the air,
In tongues of fragrance woven with a lover's care.
Each bloom becomes a letter in love's ancient script,
Speaking wisdom deeper than our hearts have yet equipped.

The roses lean toward sunlight, as hearts toward embrace,
While dew turns into gold beneath the dawn's first grace.
These moments, rich with meaning, need no words to say,
The truth that blooming hearts confess in quiet sway.

Love is hearing a song and
Suddenly thinking of them.

Cartography

Mapping uncharted territories with trembling fingers and whispered questions.

Tu es ma Belle

Tu es ma belle, my morning's grace,
Ma puce, you light my every space.
Tu es mon coeur, steady, strong, and true,
Ma chérie, for you, I'd write a song or two.

Tu es ma vie, you dance in my heart,
Ma douce, from dawn 'til dark we never part.
Tu es mon âme, so pure and clear,
Ma tendre, my joy when you are near.

Your laughter rings like rare champagne,
Your smile, a gift that soothes all pain.
With you, each moment feels brand new—
In your embrace, life doth renew.

Your Charismatic Light

Your gentle magnetism draws hearts near,
In life's swift theatre, I watch you move,
With timeless grace, unmarked by year.

At meals, you savour all that's dear,
Each moment treasured, each joy to prove—
Your gentle magnetism draws hearts near.

I see you listen, intent and clear,
Your patience lets each soul improve,
With timeless grace, unmarked by year.

Your words, like petals, soft yet sheer,
Fall strong and sure in wisdom's groove—
Your gentle magnetism draws hearts near.

In quiet strength, your light so pure,
No false veneer could misconstrue,
With timeless grace, unmarked by year.

Your path unique, your love so true,
Each second gifted, each heart to soothe—
Your gentle magnetism draws hearts near,
With timeless grace, unmarked by year.

Love is the only thing that
Makes waiting feel like time well spent.

Language

Learning to speak in the dialect of your heart—
a tongue I somehow already know.

Her Birthday

In December sweet sentiments flow,
In an ode my love , a tale to show.
Loved she might be, yet unaware,
In the garden of hearts, a secret to bear.

Strong as the oak, with roots in the ground,
Yet a gentle breeze through branches found.
A fragile part, in the core concealed,
In strength, a tender soul revealed.

Roses white, her favorites declare,
Symbols of love, she might not wear.
Enigmatic whispers in the air,
A mystery, a puzzle, beyond compare.

Educator's wisdom, a beacon bright,
Navigating realms with strength and light.
Eternal love, a melody to hum,
In the symphony of hearts, she might become.

On this December day, my verses swirl,
For her, the girl, loved in an unknowing world.

Let It Go

In shadows deep, my love's faint ember glows,
Like a withered rose, soft petals, my heart's throes.
Silken threads of longing weave a tale,
Unraveling my dreams in the seas' forlorn sail.

The question unanswered, a mournful plea,
Through corridors of time, a haunting spree.
My clockwork heart, with gears rusted, worn,
A melody of sorrow, once proudly borne.

In my garden of thought, roses weep,
Thorns of regret in memories deep.
A Mockingbird's song in the moonlit night,
Tunes my requiem for love's lost flight.

Avoidance, a maze of mirrors cracked,
Reflections distorted, fears intact.
My silent plea, behind a tear-streaked face,
Unheard, unseen, love's grand parade's disgrace.

Let it go—this dirge in the pouring rain,
Each drop a teardrop, each one my pain.
The mantra echoes 'neath a starless sky,
As the moon weeps with my lonesome sigh.

Not all discarded—some scars remain,
Etched deep within, like relentless rain.
Life's trees shed leaves, sorrow's flow,
Bare branches whisper my future of woe.

In this release, a funeral pyre's dance,
Burning echoes of love's lost romance.
New chapters rise from the ashes' trance,
Yet, love's ghost lingers, a melancholy glance.

May joy rise like a phoenix from the ash,
In the garden of healing, where sorrows clash.
Embrace the release—a mournful song,
As nightingales weep, and my heart sings along.

Love turns the simplest things—text messages, glances,
the way they say your name—into poetry.

Translation

Your silences, your laughter,
your touch—a text I study daily.

Passion's Embrace

In your loving hold, our lips entwine,
Passion unleashed, desires intertwine.
Eyes aflame with love's radiant gleam,
In wild streams of ardour, we redeem.

Your warm, tender arms encircle me tight,
Our souls find pure delight in each touch's light.
Silken tresses cascade, a veil so fine,
Caressing my face, as love's fire align.

No chaste, cold kiss for us to share,
Love devoid of fervour, timidly declared.
No saintly bliss, ethereal and pure,
But a love untamed, like a dove's allure.

Give me love unbounded, free from constraint,
Defying judgment, ignoring complaint.
With your vibrant body, ablaze with youth,
My heart ignites, lost in love's truth.

So, moistened lips, sweetly meet mine,
Scented with ruby sips, like aged wine.
Declare boldly, under southern skies,
Our souls and bodies eternally tied.

Embrace me firmly, in your arms of might,
As pale stars witness, shining through the night.
Together, we'll live with youthful glee,
In symphonies of ecstasy, forever free.

Her Rhythmic Soul

A sensory being, dancing with delight,
An essence radiating joy, a captivating sight.
Delicious beyond compare, a feast for the soul,
In books read, hidden meanings take their toll.

Within her lies power, a flickering light,
Inspired by rhythms of both day and night.
From west coast swing to hip hop's vibrant groove,
Jazz and ballet guide, graceful movements soothe.

Breaking boundaries, exploring even more,
In breakdance, finding freedom—an untamed roar.
The flamenco, with its fiery devotion,
Holds her heart, true emotion in motion.

Falling for passion, the pain it reveals,
Expressions of longing, each movement conceals.
Her soul ignited, speaking to the very core,
In elegant chicness, her energy lights the floor.

Touched by the senses, each step conveyed,
Ever the dancer, presence setting all ablaze.
Metaphors swirl, a mystical art,
In structured stanzas, the story of a poetic heart.

Love doesn't always make sense.
But that's half the fun.

Roots

Two separate trees whose roots intertwine
beneath the surface.

Dancing Through Difference

Direct as dawn, she probes the world anew,
A beacon bright, her questions cutting through.
Perceptive soul, she feels each ebb and flow,
Creative currents in her mind aglow.

Her spirit dances, free from doubt or guise,
Unconscious grace, a joy to realise.
She lights the room before she enters in,
Her energy, a force that can't be pinned.

In blissful kiss, when right connection's found,
Her patience sees beyond the here and now.
Forthright and brave, she faces what may come,
Maturing mind, to wisdom's call succumbs.

An English rose, in feature and in face,
She swims through life with feline-like grace.
For human rights and nature's verdant health,
She stands, a champion of greater wealth.

With humour keen and laughter in her eyes,
She rides life's ponies, though they buck and rise.
In neurodiversity's vibrant hues,
She finds the strength in all her points of view.

Days Upon Days

Time flows like water through my fingertips,
While silence holds back words upon my lips.
The days stretch out, then pool like morning dew,
These days upon days, keeping me from you.

Each moment crawls through hours thick and slow,
Like northern winters wrapped in endless snow.
The days stack up like pages never read,
These days upon days, words left unsaid.

Messages sent float in empty space,
Each passing day at such a glacial pace.
Time bends and warps in strange and lonely ways,
These days upon days upon endless days.

The clock hand moves with cruel indifference now,
While patience teaches me its art somehow.
Through twilight thoughts and dawn's uncertain haze,
These days upon days upon days upon days.

Until at last, fate's gentle hand arrives,
Like northern lights that dance across our skies.
The waiting ends, as destiny displays
How love survives these days upon days.

Now here we stand, time's puzzle rearranged,
By all these days that passed while hearts unchanged.
And looking back, I smile at time's delays -
Those days upon days that led me back to you.

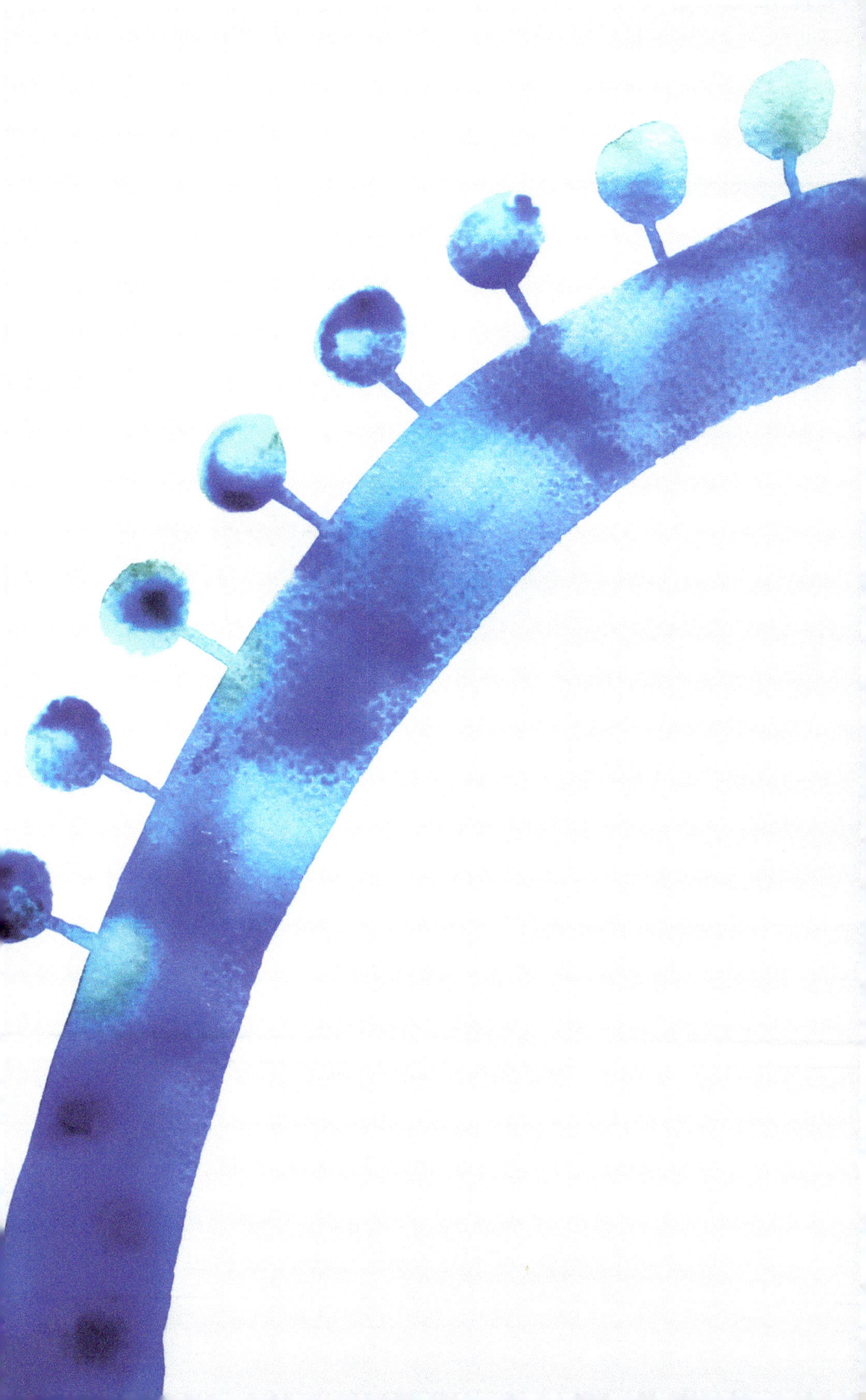

Love, once felt,
Never really leaves—it just echoes.

Weather

Learning to dance in storms, to find shelter in each
other, to be sunshine when needed.

Unrequited

Drifting through twilight, a wistful gleam so rare,
Like autumn leaves in evening's gentle flight.
He treasures their bond with reverent care,
Yet unrequited love dims his inner light.

In shadows he lingers, watching from afar,
As she, beloved, glows ever bright.
A bitter truth pierces like a falling star,
Leaving him lost in love's relentless night.

Perhaps it's time to seek dawn's embrace,
To mend his spirit in morning's rays.
In another's eyes, he may find that grace
To lead his heart through hope's untrodden ways.

No longer bound to this one-sided flame,
His heart will open to a different song.
Their friendship, pure, untouched by pain,
Endures beyond where lost dreams belong.

In time, these shadows will yield to light,
As wisdom guides him to tomorrow's shore.
Their bond preserved, a treasure bright,
While new love waits beyond hope's closing door.

Not Sorry For Love

I'm sorry for hiding a dark past, my dear,
For the shadows I concealed, fueling your fear.
I apologise for the lies that tainted the truth,
For the walls I built, keeping secrets aloof.

I'm sorry for being afraid to confide,
For holding back with my heart locked inside.
I should have been honest, open, and true,
But fear stole my voice when I needed my cue.

I'm sorry for not sharing the trials I faced—
Jail, the military, battles long traced.
The hospital stays that weathered my soul,
Forgive me for silence that left you cold.

But know this, my love—I am not sorry for
Loving you deeply, for wanting you more.
For caring with all of my strength and my light,
For striving each day to make wrong into right.

I'm not sorry for yearning to stand by your side,
To cherish, to honour, to walk as your guide.
Through sorrow, through joy, through loss and through gain,
My love will not falter; it will not wane.

So take these words as my heart's true plea,
For forgiveness, for trust—please, hear me.
I'm sorry for pain and the trust I impaired,
But my love for you is real—forever, beyond compare.

Love isn't like a cake with only so many pieces to share.
The more you give, the more there is.

Gardens

Patience in tending, wonder in witnessing
what blooms between us.

Our Continental Drift

Once we were Pangaea—whole and vast,
Until earth's deepest pulse urged change.
Now we drift as continents must.
From our core, new mountains rise
Between these widening seas,
Each shore carved by what divides us.

Through autumn mists and winter's sharpened air,
When frost etches memories on windowpanes—
Each one distinct, each a story carved in ice—
I watch our shores reshape themselves.

Like a torch-bearer passing through darkness,
Or a lighthouse keeper tending a great flame,
I stand at my post, watching your distant coast
Across waters that once were land we shared.
New seas fill the space between our shores,
Each wave carrying messages of what remains.

I'm not choosing familiar nearness,
Nor the cold comfort of total separation,
But this ocean-space between—
Where tectonic forces shape new geographies,
Neither joined nor truly apart but transformed,
Where echoes of ancient mountains still resonate
In the bedrock of both our lands.

Even now, as our coastlines settle into their new shapes,
Trading winds across the waters that divide us,
I see how life adapts and thrives;
Your forests green against distant cliffs,
Your seasons turning in their own time.

We were shaped by the same forces,
Now I watch your landscape flourish
Across these waters we didn't choose—
A divide, yes, but also a connection.
And though we cultivate separate shores,
We share the same stars, the same moon's pull,
Our tides rising and falling in ancient rhythm.

Love is rarely talked about, but often,
it's what validates a good person.

Resistance

The paradox of love: how pulling away
can bring us closer.

Dreams Beneath Northern Skies

In quiet thought, your presence softly stays,
Like northern lights that cast their mystic rays.
In whispered dreams of what may yet unfold,
Your soul calls to mine, a story untold.

Though miles apart, you linger close, it seems,
Your laughter dances softly through my dreams.
Each message shared, a beacon in the night,
A star that guides me with its steady light.

No touch we've shared, but hearts entwine, it's true—
In spirit's realm, I am bound close to you.
In spaces where our souls are free to soar,
We dance beneath the northern lights once more.

Each word we speak builds bridges through the air,
Each confession deepens what we both share.
Your essence fills my thoughts with gentle grace,
While hope constructs its castles in this place.

Perhaps one day our paths will intertwine,
Where northern stars complete the grand design.
Until that day, I'll treasure dreams like gold,
These moments when your presence feels so bold.

For now, I drift in endless possibilities,
As hopes ascend like autumn's whispered pleas.
My heart beats stronger with the thought of you,
In dreams of love that blossom, pure and true.

Love makes you want to sing, dance, write poetry,
buy Walnut Whips, and act really silly.
Love is powerful like that.

Repair

The quiet art of mending what breaks
without hiding the scars.

The Perfect Mistake

Men don't just think—they overthink with care;
Each gift becomes a chess game played in mind:
"She mentioned roses…" drifts upon the air,
The memory leaves specifics far behind.

The mental notes pile up in tangled heaps,
That coffee chat from Tuesday fades with time—
Was it this or that? The memory sleeps,
While guessing games become a paradigm.

Like last year's perfume choice, that finest feat:
"Chanel!" you thought you heard with such élan,
Not knowing she'd called "Michelle!" across to greet
Her friend amid the bustling restaurant.

Or that bouquet of lilies, tall and proud,
That sent her sneezing through the waiting crowd—
"But darling, just last week you loved them all!"
The words ring hollow as your spirits fall.

Each purchase comes with hours of research done,
The browser holds its secrets: "flower guides,"
"What roses mean" and "which colours stun,"
While roses shift from love to wounded pride.

The florist sees you pacing day by day,
Until analysis paralysis sets in—
"Perhaps I'll wait until I'm sure," you say,
While options multiply, yet none will win.

But here's the twist that makes it all worthwhile:
These perfect failures, planned with loving care,
Create a better story, mile by mile,
Than any flawless gift could hope to share.

Second-guess each hint she drops your way—
These almost-perfect gifts, these near-miss views
Build stories that we'll cherish day by day.

For in your worried, wonderful attempt
To get it absolutely right this time,
You've given something better: evidence
That love makes overthinking quite sublime.

So keep your mental notebooks, scan for clues,
Perhaps love's gift is not to get things right,
But stumble sweetly toward its endless light.

A Final Note on Love's Action
It's not the thought that counts, but thought that moves—
The courage to translate feeling into form.

For in each gesture, each imperfect choice,
Love finds its voice.
To move on instinct, follow fleeting words—
That's where love's essence lives and breathes and grows.

Love, as the Beatles said, 'Love Me Do.'
I haven't got a clue what they meant,
but it sounds good—exactly like love itself.

Resilience

Not the absence of storms but the strength to weather them—together, always together.

Secret Yawning

The dating profiles glow with hope divine,
As train sets circle through their pristine tracks,
Plus football shirts, so pressed in perfect line,
And vintage comics stacked in plastic packs.

We girls must hone this most essential art
(A skill that dating veterans must gain);
The art of yawning with closed lips, so smart,
While bright eyes shine through stories of their train.

Through tales of model planes that fill the shelf,
Through fantasy teams tracked with pristine care,
Through gaming chairs that cost more than oneself,
Through crypto gains that vanished into thin air—
So past these yawns that no one ever shows,
Will someone make our hearts beat fast? Who knows?!

Love is like being in a dark room and
someone turns on the light
—and it stays on.

Echoes

Years later, still discovering new chambers in this house we've built with our hearts.

You Pause Me

I live
  forever
    in new
      Pauses

When you pause
  I breathe
    deeper
      Believing

in the space
  between
    you
      and
        I

where emotions
  retrieve
    themselves
      from depths
        I didn't know
        I had

finding
  those moments
    you leave me
      suspended
        in time
          Paused

metaphysical
  ephemeral
    eternal
      Pauses

you
  pause
    me
      my
        beloved

and in these spaces
  between breaths
    between thoughts
      between moments
        I find
          You

in whispers
  of tomorrow
    where time
      dissolves
        into our
          infinite
            Pause

She paused me ...

Love is what makes you want to create
the memories you'll never forget.

Reflection

In your eyes at sixty, I still see the person
I fell for at twenty.

The English Exit

L'Entente Cordiale, that gentle accord,
Where each points to the other when slipping abroad.
"Filer à l'anglaise," the French sweetly say,
While we blame the French for our slipping away.

In Parisian salons or London's grand halls,
Both sides perfect their vanishing calls:
"Just stepping out" meets "Je dois partir"—
Two cultures united in swift disappear.

When dating apps cross the wide Channel seas,
Both sides ghost with identical ease.
No matter the language of love that we speak,
We've mastered the art of the discrete retreat.

Some say it started with old Henry Eight,
Who made swift exits rather his trait.
The French kings replied with equal finesse:
"L'état c'est moi"—then gone, more or less.

So whether we bow or whether we curtsey,
Whether Dover or Calais makes us all mercy,
The art of departure knows no frontiers—
Just two nations perfect in causing arrears.

Perhaps that's why friendship has lasted so long:
We're both rather good at the slip-away song.
Each blaming the other with dignified grace,
While sharing the same sophisticated space.

French Exit, Bradford Return

You said we'd spoken—was it a year?
If I had recalled, I'd swear it was clear.
But memories fade like ink in the rain,
Or maybe I'm cursed to forget and retain.

I did not know the name or the words,
But one photo lingered—unshaken, unstirred.
A city-lit mirror, a snapshot of you,
A moment in time I somehow still knew.

A French exit, you left without trace,
No note, no goodbye—just vanished in place.
Yet here you are, like déjà vu,
Reappearing, familiar—but startlingly new.

Love is a precious gift.
That's why it's always felt in the present.

Continuance

Love cycles through seasons, always finding its way
back to perpetual spring.

'The Light You Bring

Love, your presence blooms like dawn on tranquil seas,
A quiet glow that turns my night to day.
With every glance, my heart, you set it free.

The air grows still as if the world agrees,
And time itself lets shadows fade away.
Love, your presence blooms like dawn on tranquil seas.

Your laugh, like summer's warmth upon the trees,
Illuminates my path—a golden ray.
With every glance, my heart, you set it free.

When we're apart, I gather memories,
Each moment treasured in time's bright display.
Love, your presence blooms like dawn on tranquil seas.

For in you, I find the part of me that frees
My soul to soar beyond the bounds of day.
With every glance, my heart, you set it free.

When you arise, a brave new future breathes;
These feelings find their simple way to say:
Love, your presence blooms like dawn on tranquil seas;
With every glance, my heart is set free.

To My Poem For You

I hope you liked the meter and the rhyme,
The structured words, arranged with great intent,
For one alone could never quite present
The thoughts I've had of you, time after time.

But now you say you don't deserve this chime—
A claim, I fear, that logic must prevent,
For if unworthy you, what's heaven-sent
In beauty, grace, and words that seek to climb?

Yet still, lest I seem much too grave a poet,
I'll say in jest (and mean it all the same),
That verse should never make its writer weep.
So, if the first one made your heart bestow it
A smile or two, I claim no weighty fame—
Except, of course, in thoughts of you, quite deep.

The Recycling Crisis

If you should spurn these verses that I penned,
I face a poet's strangest predicament—
A name-specific rhyme I cannot mend
Without some creative management.

For Lisa cannot change to Jane or Sue,
Without destroying rhythm, rhyme, and grace.
(And truthfully, between just me and you,
The internet's recycling is a disgrace!)

So here I sit with verses specialised,
A craftsman with a tool too finely made.
Perhaps I should have generalised—
Used darling, love, or some such safer trade.

But no! For though this risks poetic waste,
Your name's the verse that cannot be replaced.

This Tale Will Never Get Paroled

Oh, Calliope, muse of endless rhyme,
Your guidance shapes the verse that paints the skies.
With every word, I trace our fates through time,
And in each line, your influence never dies.

Your name, dear Lisa, in my verse must stand—
A constant echo, born of rhyme and light.
No fleeting words can change it, take command,
For yours alone can make these lines take flight.

And though I face the crisis of my rhyme,
I'll never fault, nor shall I relent.
For Lisa's tale will never get paroled—
The story's trapped in ink and will not bend.

Each line I write, I cannot yet undo,
Your name remains, again for me to you.
This regional short note
Seems somehow to be becoming an epic tale,
And when I consider that, I must say—
That wouldn't be such a fail!

Time's Sacred Scroll

Oh Clio, pause with me in reverent thought,
As Time's great wheel turns moments into lore.
These verses, each with careful passion wrought,
Now paint a history we can't ignore.

From dawn-lit seas where first my heart took flight,
Through recycled thoughts and names enshrined,
Each response has led us to this height
Where poetry and truth become entwined.

In silence now, between each line we pause,
As wonder fills these spaces we create.
Dear Lisa's words become such sacred cause—
The way she pauses sets our verse and fate.

For in these pauses, time stands clear and true:
You pause my heart, and paused, I am with you.

A Song of Times Past and Present

Euterpe, make my verses sing tonight,
As melodies flow soft through Lisa's name.
Like music that no silence can reclaim,
Each pause between us brings fresh notes to light.

As melodies flow soft through Lisa's name,
Like dawn that once lit up my tranquil seas,
Each pause between us brings fresh notes to light,
While sacred scrolls unfurl on Time's sweet breeze.

Like dawn that once lit up my tranquil seas,
These verses, wrought with passion, cannot bend,
While sacred scrolls unfurl on Time's sweet breeze,
As heart to heart our rhythms sweetly flow.

These verses, wrought with passion, cannot bend,
Each moment caught in songs we freely share,
As heart to heart our rhythms sweetly flow,
Like stars that dance in evening's tender air.

Each moment caught in songs we freely share,
The music of your presence sets me free,
Like stars that dance in evening's tender air,
In gentle time that guides my heart to see.

The music of your presence sets me free,
Like music that no silence can reclaim,
In gentle time that guides my heart to see—
Will our souls find their pathway to this flame?

Love is the only thing that can make
you cry and still feel good.

Left And Right

Left and right, an endless tide,
Profiles flash, hopes collide.
Swipe left, swipe left, again I sigh—
Will Cupid's arrow ever fly?

Then suddenly, amidst the crowd,
A sight that made me gasp aloud:
Those emerald eyes with depth so rare,
Like Lauren Bacall's magnetic stare.

A classic beauty, dark and bright,
(At last, a reason to swipe right!)
With grace that hints of Hollywood,
And vintage charm that's understood.

In this digital carousel,
Where profiles spin and stories tell,
Most photos blur and fade away,
But yours made Time itself delay.

You asked me why I chose to stop,
(My heart did quite a little hop.)
Well, since you asked, I'll tell you true:
There's something timeless about you.

Like silver screen stars of yesteryear,
Your gaze has made me pause right here.
Though dating apps may seem absurd,
I'm glad I swiped the way I did!

And if this poem seems over-bold,
(Or frankly, just a bit too old),
Well, rhymes are rare in Tinder chat—
So take a chance and answer back!

The Match!

I've tried them all, oh yes I have,
Each dating app's distinctive salve:
Elite Singles (what a jest!),
Where everyone's "above the rest."

On Bumble where the ladies lead,
On Hinge where stories should proceed,
eHarmony with endless tests —
Each promising romantic quests.

But here on Tinder, what's this sight?
That green-eyed grace swiped back tonight!
My Lauren Bacall lookalike
Has deemed my poetic words alright!

From all the apps I've swiped before,
Through profiles by the endless score,
Who knew my rhyming late at night
Would finally make a match feel right?

Now what to say? Keep up the verse?
(Could poetry make matters worse?)
But wait — she's typing! Hold your breath!
Is this a match to end my depth?

The Local Dilemma

That match became a chat so sweet,
Then came the words: "Let's plan to meet!"
"Keep London for another day,
Let's lunch up North," I heard her say.

The Shibden Mill—well, it's so near,
(A tennis ball's toss and you're there!)
But many at the bar would see,
And word would spread like wildfire—me!

"He's got a date!" they'd surely cry,
As every local wandered by.
Old blokes would wink, the girls would grin,
Before we'd even touched a gin!

She lives just four miles down the way,
(In Yorkshire terms, that's next door, eh?)
But finding somewhere neither's known
Is harder than you'd think back home!

In London, we could strangers be,
In Yorkshire—well, just wait and see!
For every pub holds tales to tell,
And locals love to wish you well!

Perhaps we need a cunning plan,
To dodge the gossips if we can?
But then again, why sneak or hide?
Let Yorkshire hearts beam full of pride.

Double Doors, Double Lives

The Shibden Mill has entrances two,
(A cunning plan was coming through!)
Restaurant right, and left the bar,
I thought my scheme would work thus far!

I snuck in through the dining door,
While she approached the public floor,
But Yorkshire fate had other plans,
As through the bar her friends began:

"Hey there! Come join us!" came their call,
(My careful planning took a fall),
She caught my eye across the space,
A panic flashing 'cross her face.

"Who's that you're meeting?" friends inquired,
"Oh, just a business thing," transpired!
I had to smile - quick thinking there,
A cover story we could share!

Through bar to restaurant, glances flew,
Both playing roles completely new.
"Just work," we'd say if asked to share,
While secret smiles crossed through the air!

In Yorkshire pubs, the walls have eyes,
But sometimes that brings sweet surprise:
Two people, same creative mind,
Both leaving local truth behind!

The Gentleman's Guide

When choosing seats, I knew the way,
(A gentleman's role to play),
To pull her chair, to guide her there,
Her back kept from the thoroughfare.

The room before her, hers to scan,
While I faced only her—the plan.
(For men, we know, are simple souls,
Distracted when the beauty strolls!)

Let her watch the world drift by,
While I keep focus, eye to eye.
No wandering glance would break our chat,
A gentleman knows the sense in that.

They say chivalry's had its day,
But small things still can pave the way:
A pulled-out chair, a thoughtful seat,
Can make a Yorkshire date complete.

These gentle arts aren't played for show,
But let her quiet comfort grow.
For romance blooms in subtle ways,
Through little acts on Yorkshire days.

The Meet

She spoke of Oxford's hallowed halls,
(Well, Oxford Brooks, when truth recalls!)
While I, with tales perhaps too bold,
Of swimming glory had foretold.

"International champion, you say?"
She raised an eyebrow, clear as day.
"Synchronised solo?" came her jest,
As both our 'reps' failed their test.

Our representatives had led,
These dating profiles, carefully fed
With half-truths wrapped in hopeful shine,
Now crumbling over Yorkshire wine.

But as our laughter filled the air,
These honest moments made us share
The real souls behind the screen,
Not who we'd claimed, but who we'd been!

For dating apps may start the game,
With profiles polished into fame,
But Yorkshire truth will have its say,
As real folk meet on real days!

Tuscan Sunflower

Along the winding paths through ancient hills,
Where cypress stands like sentinels of stone,
She found beyond the dancing, endless rills,
A lone sunflower, proud and unrestrained.

Taller than all its kin in golden throng,
Its petals burned in the dawn's molten light,
While others bowed to the winds all day long,
It stood — unshaken, regal in its height.

Perhaps it spoke to something in her core—
This bold bloom, steadfast in the sun's embrace,
Apart, yet perfect, reaching evermore,
A timeless rebel in this sacred place.

In foreign fields where golden flowers grew,
She saw herself in one that dared break through.

You Are Missing from Me

You are missing from me—
like an ocean robbed of its dancing waves,
like a night sky bereft of its diamond stars.
A hollow conch shell murmurs ancient secrets,
echoes of my former self spiral inward,
deeper than the trenches where pearls sleep—
empty, yet yearning to be whole.

If you stood here beside me,
I'd taste the salt on your lips,
smell the brine in your hair,
let the sea breeze weave stories between us—
stories of depths we never fathomed,
of coral gardens we never tended.
But your heart: you gifted it at dawn,
when the tide was highest,
and in return,
I surrendered mine—
an open wound blooming like anemones in darkened water.

Without you,
the air thins to vapour, leaving my lungs raw.
Light dissolves into muted watercolours;
the world hums its vacant melody,
rippling outward into silence.
I exist as scattered fragments of sea glass—
edges smoothed by time's patient tides,
yet brittle as sand dollars bleached by endless sun.

You are missing from me—
as if my soul forgot its vibrant dance,
as if morning misplaced its golden promise,
leaving whispered twilight
and footprints in wet sand
claimed by the tide.
Each wave erases another memory,
pulling moments back to the deep.

You are missing from me still—
like breath held underwater,
like shells waiting for the tide to return them home.
Yet even in this absence, your shadow lingers,
a faint whisper in the undertow,
a rhythm my heart cannot forget—
constant as the moon commands the waves,
eternal as salt on every shore.

Acta non verba, sed semper in amore.

Actions, not words, but always with love.

Evans Webb

LOVE POEMS
First published by Evans Webb
© Creag McMillian and Heidi Sturgess 2025

The right of Creag McMillan and Heidi Sturgess as author and illustrator of this book has been asserted by them in accordance with the Copyright, Designs and Patent Act 1988.

All rights reserved. No part of this book may be reproduced, transmitted, or stored in an information retrieval system in any form or by any means, graphic, electronic or mechanical, including photocopying, taping and recording, without prior written permission from the publisher.

ISBN 9780993148033

www.evanswebb.co.uk

www.ingramcontent.com/pod-product-compliance
Lightning Source LLC
Chambersburg PA
CBHW051550010526
44118CB00022B/2655